Don't Sell Me Short

Judith A. Bosley

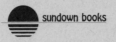 sundown books

SIGNAL HILL

ATTENTION READERS: We would like to hear what you think about our books. Please send your comments or suggestions to:

The Editors
Signal Hill Publications
P.O. Box 131
Syracuse, NY 13210-0131

• • •

This book is fiction. The author invented the names, people, places, and events. If any of them are like real places, events, or people (living or dead), it is by chance.

SIGNAL HILL

© 1988, 1990 Signal Hill Publications
A publishing imprint of Laubach Literacy International

10 9 8 7 6 5 4 3

ISBN 0-88336-205-8

Illustrations by Patti DiCarlo
Cover design by Chris Steenwerth
Cover photo by Hal Silverman Studio

Signal Hill is a not-for-profit publisher. The proceeds from the sale of this book support the national and international programs of Laubach Literacy International.

PRINTED WITH
SOYINK™

This book was printed on 100% recycled paper which contains 50% post-consumer waste.

Table of Contents

Chapter 1

A Losing Battle

"School is very hard for Richard. He is such a nice boy, and he tries hard. But he can't keep up with the others. We work with him, but he needs special help. Try to read to him a lot this summer."

Mrs. Rose, Richard's fourth grade teacher, took off her glasses as she spoke. "Don't give up on him, Mrs. Cook."

Richard had been nine when Mrs. Rose was his teacher. Now he's 19, thought Carol, his mother. Poor Richard. Things never did get better, did they, honey? She was holding her handsome son's high school graduation picture. His sweet smile made her want to cry.

"My little big boy," Carol said softly. "What will you do when I'm gone?"

Carol was dying. She had fought hard, but the cancer was winning. Today, the battle seemed too hard.

The letter had come from the Army. It read, "Dear Mr. and Mrs. Cook: Your son Richard is being discharged today. His test scores were too low for our standards. We do not feel that he can do the work. We wish Richard good luck in the future." The letter was signed, "Commander Robert Stern, United States Army."

Carol and Dan Cook had tried hard with their three children. Pam and Steve were now out on their own and doing well. Pam was a nurse, and Steve was away at college. Richard was the youngest. The Cooks had hoped the Army might be the answer for him. They had hoped he would find work there that he liked and could do. The letter ended their hopes and plans.

Richard had been gone for a month. He had joined the Army even before school was out. They had been very proud at his going-away party. But in her heart, Carol knew it wouldn't work.

Richard had trouble with reading. Often, he didn't understand exactly what he was told. She could make him understand. Other people couldn't or didn't take the time. She had prayed to live long enough to help him get a start.

Suddenly, a wave of pain made Carol stop thinking of Richard. She dropped the picture and fought back again.

Her husband, Dan, came into the room. "Is it bad, honey?" he asked. She didn't answer him. She was pounding on her bed with her hands. He went to telephone the doctor. Dr. Rogers came later and gave her a shot. Finally, she slept.

Richard came home from the Army just a few days later. He went to his mother's room. "Hi, Mom. How are you doing?" He had a cheerful, happy smile, as always.

She smiled weakly at him. "I'm glad you are home, honey."

"Yeah, well, the Army didn't want me," he said. "I couldn't do anything fast enough for them. The sergeant said I'm a loser."

"No!" Carol raised herself up in her bed. "No, you are not a loser! I don't care what the sergeant said. Richard, you are a winner. You are gentle and kind. You care about people. You will find a job that's good for you. Promise me that you will keep that smile. Promise me you will keep looking and trying. Promise me, Richard."

Carol fell back on her pillow then. Richard's father took his arm and said, "Come, son." He led Richard out of the room. "Son, your mother is much worse now," he told him. "We are not going to have her much longer."

"What do you mean, Dad?" asked Richard. "Isn't Mom going to get well?"

"I'm afraid not, son. Don't you see how thin and sick she is? Dr. Rogers said she couldn't last *this* long. She has been waiting to see you again."

Tears started to roll down Richard's cheeks. He had not understood before. He went back to Carol's room. He dropped to his knees beside her bed. "Mom, you aren't going to leave me, are you?" he cried.

She pulled his head down to her pillow. "Richard, you are a man now. All mothers have to die and leave their sons. My pain is very bad now, and I want to go. Try to understand. Soon, I will be in heaven. I will watch over you. I will watch to see that you keep that smile. If bad things happen, remember that I love you."

She was too tired to speak anymore. Richard took her hand in his. "Go to sleep, Mom. I'll sit here with you." She smiled at him and closed her eyes.

All through the night, Richard sat there. His sister Pam came, and then his brother Steve. Dr. Rogers came and left again. Pam sometimes left the room, but Richard never did.

Finally, it started to get light. As the sun came up, Richard looked out the window. He said, "It's morning, Mom. The night is over." His words woke Dan, who was sleeping in a

chair. Dan looked at Carol. He ran for the telephone.

"Mom, wake up, it's morning," Richard said. But she was very still. She wasn't breathing. "Oh, Mom," he whispered. "Oh, Mom."

* * *

The little church was full. The Cooks had a large family and many friends. They all came to tell Carol good-bye. She had been sick for nearly two years. She had been very brave.

Those sitting in the church were remembering Carol Cook. Through her tears, Pam remembered her mother. She remembered a special day.

* * *

Pam had said, "Mom, I want to go on to school. I want to become a nurse."

"Good, Pam," Carol had said. "I'll be so proud of you. I always wanted to be a nurse myself."

"So why don't you go to school with me?" asked Pam.

"I'm too old," laughed Carol. "Besides, we don't have the money. We can barely afford to send you to school and then Steve, too."

"You are not too old," Pam replied. "Women go back to school every day. You would make a great nurse. And you could use the money that Grandma Gentry left you."

10

Carol's mother had died quite young, when Carol was a girl. She had left Carol an inheritance. "That money is for Richard," Carol said quickly.

"You wouldn't have to spend much," Pam said. "I could live at home. We could drive to class together. That way, it wouldn't cost as much. Mom, let's do it! We can study together. I know it would make Dad happy. What do you say?"

Carol didn't answer for a minute. Pam's idea did make sense. The town they lived in was just outside a city. There was a good nursing school in the city.

"Pam, you have no idea how tempted I am. I can't believe it," said Carol. "But I'm going to say yes. I think this is a dream come true!"

The dream did come true, but only for Pam. They had been halfway through nursing school. Then her mother had her yearly checkup, and the doctor found a tumor. It was the same thing that had happened to Grandma Gentry, Carol's mother.

* * *

Now, Pam sat at her mother's funeral, crying bitter tears. The same disease had taken both her mother and grandmother. It wasn't fair.

Dan sat quietly in the church pew. Carol had suffered terribly. He did not wish her back.

Steve sat with his arm around his father. "She was such a wonderful wife and mother," said Dan.

"Yes. She was, Dad," said Steve. "The best. We were all very lucky."

Richard sat between Pam and Grandpa Gentry. Richard was not crying. He was smiling. He heard the singing and prayers. It made him feel happy.

Pam looked at him through her tears. She whispered, "Richard, how can you sit there, grinning? What must people think of you?"

He replied, "I promised Mom I would smile, and I will."

Pam did not understand him at all. She didn't have much patience with him, either.

After it was all over and Grandpa Gentry had gone back home to the city, the Cook family was alone. Richard went out into the yard and sat under a tree. Steve looked out the window at him. "Dad, I'm very concerned about Richard. What will happen to him now, with Mom gone? I'm his big brother, and I'd like to help him. But with school, and my being so far away—"

"You and Pam both have your own problems, Steve," said his father. "Your mother left him some money. And I will help him all I can."

"Mom saved that money from Grandma Gentry all these years," said Pam. "She only spent a small part of it on herself for nursing school. She always told us it was for Richard. I just hope he doesn't waste it."

"I'll take care of it," said her father. "I'll help him get started at something."

Chapter 2
The Plan

After Carol's funeral, things began to settle down. Richard drove Steve to the train to go back to school. Steve hugged him and said, "Good-bye, little brother. Take care of Dad." Then he was gone. Pam soon returned to her apartment near the hospital where she worked. It was just in the nearby city, but she seldom came home.

Richard lived with his father. He had grown up on the quiet street. He had played in the vacant lot next door. He was used to the neighborhood, and he was happy there.

Richard tried hard to please his father. He fixed their food and washed the dishes. He mowed the lawn and trimmed the bushes. He even sewed on buttons and mended their clothes. Carol had taught him to do many things.

Dan was very lonely. He missed Carol terribly. Everything in every room reminded him of her. Most of all, Richard reminded him of her. He was tall, blond, and slim like Carol. He was gentle and soft-spoken like his mother. He even cooked some of the same foods Carol had cooked. Richard had spent a lot of time with his mother.

But Dan and Richard had never been close. Dan couldn't share his pain with his son.

Steve was different. He had always been a bright boy. He was doing well in school. Dan was very proud of him. They also shared a common hobby—ham radio. Steve had a radio set at school.

Late at night, Richard would hear Dan on the radio. He would be talking to Steve or to strangers far away. Richard wished he could be close to his father, as Steve was. He felt very alone without his mother.

While Dan was away at work, Richard helped Grandpa G. The Cook children had always called Carol's father Grandpa G. He lived in the city, but he owned the vacant lot next to their house. He also owned the house beyond the vacant lot.

Grandpa G. was a carpenter. He had bought the big house to make into apartments. The downstairs apartment was finished. An older lady was living there. Richard and Grandpa G.

worked on the upstairs. There would be two apartments upstairs.

Richard loved his Grandpa G., and Grandpa G. loved Richard. They got along very well. They told jokes and laughed together. They fixed their food and ate together. His grandfather taught Richard how to saw a board straight. He taught him how to fix windows and lay carpeting.

Best of all, Richard loved his grandfather's stories. Other people got tired of hearing the same stories over again—but not Richard. He would say, "Tell me the story about Old Babe."

Grandpa G. had kept horses on his farm. It was a long time ago. There was Old Babe and Vera. They were plow horses. Old Babe had a straw hat. Grandpa G. had made it by cutting holes for her ears. Sometimes, he would put a flower in Old Babe's hat. Richard liked that story.

Dan had been thinking about Richard's future. He knew Richard could not be like Steve. But he wanted him to be happy and on his own. He and Grandpa Gentry had a long talk.

One night, Dan and Grandpa G. sat down with Richard. "Son," said Dan, "let's make some plans for you. Your grandfather and I have an idea. How would you like to buy the apartment house from him?"

Richard stared at Dan. He had never thought about having a house of his own. "Houses cost a lot of money," said Richard.

He knew that his mother had left him some money. He didn't know how much it was. His father was keeping it for him. "Would I have enough to pay for it?" Richard asked.

"No, but you have enough to begin with," said his father. "Grandpa G. has a mortgage on the apartment house. A mortgage is a loan from the bank to buy property. And you can assume Grandpa's mortgage."

Grandpa G. interrupted to explain. "*Assume* is what banks call it when somebody else takes over paying back the mortgage."

Richard's father went on. "Here's how it would work. You give Grandpa G. some of your money for the down payment. That pays him for what he has already spent on the house. You can live in one of the apartments. You can rent out the other two. Every month, you will go to the bank. You will make your payment on the mortgage there. Grandpa G. will help you. You would have the rest of the rent money to buy food and clothes. You would also need to look for a job. And you would have to be careful with your money. Do you understand?"

"That's a neat idea," Richard answered. "And I want to buy a car. Do I have enough money for that, too?" Dan and Grandpa Gentry were surprised.

Dan looked at his son thoughtfully. Richard was a good driver and a careful one. He would need a way to get around. Dan thought about all these things. Finally, he said, "OK, we'll find a car for you, too."

Richard jumped up from the table. "Thanks a lot, Dad. Thank you, too, Gramps. I'm going to tell Dee the good news. I will have a house and car! Oh, boy!" He dashed out the front door.

Dan and Mr. Gentry looked at each other. "He will have a few hundred left, but not much," said Dan.

"I hope we're doing the right thing," said Grandpa Gentry.

"So do I," said Dan, looking worried.

Dee Spencer lived across the street. She had been Carol Cook's best friend. She liked Richard, too. She had watched him grow up. Richard waved at her through the screen door.

"Dee, I'm going to have a house and a car!"

"You're what?" said Dee.

"I'm going to buy the apartment house from Gramps with my own money. And I'm going to buy a car."

Dee couldn't help but smile at Richard. He was so excited and happy.

"I'll be your neighbor, just like always," Richard said. "I'll help you, too, Dee. I'll mow your lawn and get your groceries. It will be great!"

Then Richard jumped down off Dee's porch. He ran over to the vacant lot. He stood there and looked at the house that he would own. Dee watched him. After the first surprise of his news, she was worried, just as his father and grandfather were.

Chapter 3

A Roof and Wheels

The next week, Richard went to the bank with Grandpa G. Richard signed the papers the bank gave him to take over the mortgage on the apartment house.

Richard moved his bed and bedding into one of the two upstairs apartments. It still needed some work, but it was almost finished. He was so delighted. Everything was new and shiny. He got a small table and chairs from his father's basement. "Can I have some pots and pans and dishes, Dad?" he asked Dan.

"Take whatever you want," said his father. "I can't cook, anyhow."

"Gee, Dad. Who will cook for you with me moving out?" asked Richard.

"I don't imagine that I'll starve." Dan spoke without looking up from his paper.

"Mom always said anyone named Cook should learn how," said Richard. "That's why she taught Steve and me to cook." His father didn't look up. Richard got a box for the dishes.

When Richard had his kitchen furnished, he invited Dee over. "Well, aren't you a fine gentleman!" she remarked. "I have an old couch and chair you can use. Maybe I can find a lamp, too." Richard was very happy.

Dan came to Richard's apartment one day after work. "Come on, we'll go look for a car," he said.

"Don't you want to come in and see my place?" Richard asked.

"It's late. There isn't time if you want to buy a car. Let's go," his father said.

They drove to the used car lot nearby. The dealer had a green compact car for sale. Dan thought it was a good buy. There was also a red Buick. It was big and shiny. It had fancy wheel covers.

"Dad, I really like this Buick," said Richard.

"The compact would use less gas, and it costs less," said his father.

When the salesman heard the conversation, he spoke up. "Yes, this is a mighty fine little Buick. Low mileage, not a speck of rust. She'll hold the road well. Doesn't use much oil, if you take care of her."

"I would take good care of her, too, Dad," Richard begged. "I know how to change the oil and rotate the tires. I can keep the whitewalls clean. Let's get this one, Dad."

"Richard, the green one is a better buy," said Dan. He shook his head. He thought the flashy red car was a poor idea. And he didn't like the smile on the face of the salesman. But it was Richard's first car. He wanted him to be happy with it. Finally, he said, "OK. Drive it home." He paid the smiling salesman, and Richard had his car.

Richard had never been so busy and happy before. He visited with the nice lady who lived in the downstairs apartment. He worked with Grandpa G. on the last apartment. He raked and mowed his lawn.

Nearly every day, he spent some time cleaning and polishing his car. He would sit under the tree and admire the shine. He liked to look out his window and see it in the driveway. He was very careful whenever he was driving it.

Richard sometimes took Grandpa G. for a ride. They would go to the hardware store after tools and nails. Sometimes, they stopped for ice cream.

They were sitting, one day, at the ice cream stand, when Grandpa G. started one of his stories. He said, "Richie, did I ever tell you about my first car? She was a Model A Ford. That car was a humdinger! I nearly broke my arm twice cranking her."

"And all the pretty girls liked you," Richard said. "They wanted to ride in your car. And Grandma always said that you didn't have any money. So she married you for your car."

"Guess I must have told you that one before, huh, buddy?"

"Once or twice, Gramps. I like that one."

"Richard, you are a winner. You're a good sport and good company."

"I think you're a winner, too, Gramps," said Richard.

Chapter 4

New People, Old People

After he moved, Richard didn't see much of his father. Many nights, Dan didn't come home after work. The house would be dark. Early one morning, Richard saw his father in the driveway. He walked across the lot to say hello.

"Hi, Dad. Long time, no see. Where have you been keeping yourself?"

"I've been busy, son. I have a lot of things to take care of, and so do you." Dan got behind the wheel of his car. He started up the motor. "Take care of yourself, and don't worry about me." He backed out of the driveway and drove up the street.

Richard stood in the driveway, looking after the car. He said aloud, "Gee, Dad, I didn't mean—" Then he put his hands in his pockets. He walked slowly back across to his house. His father had never talked to him like that before. He wondered what he had said wrong. He couldn't figure out why Dan was so busy.

Each Sunday, Richard went out to buy a Sunday paper. That had been his job since he was little. Now, he brought it to Dan out of habit. Richard would take the comics section. His father would read the rest.

One Sunday, when Richard took his father the paper, there was a woman in the kitchen. She was cooking dinner. Dan said, "Mavis, this is Richard. Richard, this is Mavis Parks."

Mavis had short, very blonde, curly hair. She had on a green dress that showed off her figure, and a white apron. She wore red lipstick. Her perfume smelled good. Richard thought she was pretty.

Richard shook hands with Mavis. His mother had taught him to be polite. Then he said, "Hey, Dad, have you got a girlfriend?"

Mavis's face got very red. So did Dan's. "Richard, don't be rude," Dan said.

That hurt Richard's feelings. He hadn't meant to be rude. He was just asking a question. He sat down at the table and was very quiet. Mavis poured him a cup of coffee. He said, "Thank you." Then she sat down at the table. She sat in his mother's chair. She was cooking in his mother's kitchen. All of a sudden, Richard missed his mother a lot.

"You don't look much like your father," said Mavis.

"No, I look like my mom," replied Richard. "You're sitting in her chair."

Mavis jumped up as if the chair were hot. Her face was red again. She went to the stove to stir something.

"That wasn't necessary, Richard," said his father.

"I didn't mean to hurt her feelings, Dad. I just meant that it was Mom's place."

"Forget about the chair, Richard. Will you just forget about the damn chair!" Dan got up and left the room.

Richard sat there and watched Mavis. She didn't turn around or speak to him again. "I'd better be going now," he said. He paused by the door. No one spoke to him. Then he started off across the yard. They had not asked him to stay for dinner.

Mavis watched him cross the yard between the houses. "My, he is a strange one!" she said. "I can see why he drives you crazy." Dan came and stood beside her. His arm was around her.

"He doesn't drive me crazy, Mavis," said Dan. "He's just different. He says things just as they pop into his head. He doesn't know how they sound to others sometimes. I want you to like him, Mavis."

"All he has to do is behave himself," said Mavis. "If he minds his manners, we'll get along just fine. Now, let's have dinner. It's all ready."

* * *

Work was going very well on the last apartment. The midsummer weather made it hot work. Richard and Grandpa G. usually worked in the morning and evening. They had just the bedroom closet and some painting to finish. Then it would be ready to rent.

It was a steamy August morning. Grandpa G. had gone downstairs to cut a board. Richard was waiting to nail up the closet shelf. He heard Grandpa G. start up the stairs. He was carrying the heavy shelf board.

Then Richard heard a crash. He ran and looked down the stairway. Grandpa G. was sitting on one of the steps. He was bent over and holding his left arm. "Richard, I'm sick," he said. "Take me to the hospital."

Richard half carried his grandfather to the car. He fastened a seat belt around each of them. He eased the red Buick out onto the highway. The hospital was 10 miles away in the city. Richard drove faster than he ever had before.

"Don't worry, Gramps. I'm a good driver. I'll get you there safely," he said.

"I'm not worried, Richard. I trust you and your driving. Besides, I think we'd better hurry," he said. Then he closed his eyes and leaned back against the seat. Those were the last words he ever spoke to Richard.

Richard zoomed up to the Emergency Room door. He blew his horn loudly for help. He looked over at Grandpa G. He was very pale. A nurse ran out to the car. She ran back inside and returned with a stretcher and another nurse.

As they wheeled him into the hospital, one nurse pressed hard on his chest. They took him into the Emergency Room and closed the door. Richard paced up and down outside the door. He heard, "Stat E.R.! Stat E.R.!" over the loudspeaker. A doctor came running down the hall. He went into the Emergency Room. Very soon, he came out. "Did you bring this man in?" he asked Richard.

"Yes, I'm Richard Cook. He's my grandfather. Is he going to be all right?"

"I'm sorry, Mr. Cook. He is gone. He had a massive heart attack. There was nothing we could do."

Richard dropped down heavily on a bench. He covered his face with his shaking hands. "I drove as fast as I could to get him here," he said. He started to sob.

"You did the right thing," said the doctor. "But it was just too late. Can I call anyone for you?"

"My sister, Pam Cook, works here. Yes, please call her."

Soon, Pam came running down the hall. She had already heard the news. She was crying. Richard tried to put his arm around her. She pulled away from him.

"It's all your fault," she sobbed. "It's all your fault. That kind, wonderful old man is dead because of you. He worked himself to death for you. He never had time for Steve and me. It was always Richard, Richard, Richard. Well, now I hope you're satisfied." She turned and walked into the Emergency Room and closed the door.

Richard just stared at the closed door. He felt numb. People walked by him. Doors opened and closed, but he didn't see or hear. Finally, he got up and walked slowly back to his car.

Chapter 5

House for Sale

After his grandfather's death, Richard just lay in bed, day after day. He didn't even eat. Flies buzzed around him, and he watched them. Sometimes, there was a knock at the door. He didn't get up to answer it.

Dee Spencer was worried about him. He wasn't at the funeral. She hadn't seen him, but his car was in the driveway. She went over and knocked on his door. She had to step over a board that was lying in the stairway.

"Richard, it's Dee." No answer. "I know you're in there. Get up and let me in." Still no answer. "Young man, you come to the door this minute!" she shouted.

She heard shuffling noises inside. Richard opened the door. He wore nothing but a dirty pair of sweat pants.

"Look at you!" said Dee. "You haven't shaved or washed. And look at this place! Richard, I'm giving you one hour to get yourself cleaned up. Then you be at my house for dinner. We will talk."

Dee left then, and Richard did as he was told.

After dinner, Dee talked to him just as his mother had. She was a lot like his mother. "You can't just lie around. You have work to do. Both your mother and Grandpa G. believed in you. They believed you would keep smiling and keep trying. Richard, are you listening to me?"

He was feeling better since he had eaten. He told her what Pam had said at the hospital.

"She didn't mean it," said Dee. "When we are shocked and hurt, we say things we don't mean. You were not to blame in any way. Your grandpa loved you and loved his work. You know that, don't you?"

"Yes," he said with tears in his eyes. "But now I'm all alone. I needed Gramps, and I needed Mother. They helped me."

"I know you needed them, honey," she replied. "But they taught you many things. They taught you so that you could make it without them. Don't you see? That's the way it works. We help other people learn. Then they can go on without us. We all have to die sometime. And we all leave someone behind who has to go on alone."

They were sitting at Dee's kitchen table. They heard a "tap-tap" outside. Dee opened the front door and looked out. "Well, what the—" she said. A woman was pounding a sign in Dan Cook's yard. It said For Sale. As they watched, Mavis Parks came out the door of the house.

"Come on, Richard," said Dee. "Let's see what's going on."

Richard and Dee crossed the street. "Do you mean that Dan's house is for sale?" Dee asked Mavis.

"That's what the sign says," replied Mavis.

"He didn't tell me he was moving," said Dee.

"Does he usually tell you his business?" asked Mavis.

Dee said, "We've been friends for a long time. It seems like he would have told me."

"Well, I'll tell you," said Mavis. "He's selling the house and getting married. Then he's moving into my house." Mavis turned and walked back toward the house. "Come on, Millie," she said to the real estate lady.

Richard ran after Mavis. "What about my mother's things?" he asked.

"You'll have to talk to your father about that," Mavis said. She walked away from them to her car.

"I'll be switched!" said Dee. "Come on, Richard." They went back across the street to her house. Dee phoned Dan at work.

"Dan, this is Dee Spencer. A woman just put a For Sale sign in your yard. Mavis Parks told Richard and me that you're getting married and moving. Now, I don't care if you sell your house. And I don't care if you marry that woman. But don't you think Richard has a right to be told?"

Dee listened on the line. Then she said, "Well, I should think you would!"

Dee hung up. "Let's forget this for now, Richard. Come on with me. We're going to get you some groceries. Then I'll help you clean up your place."

Richard never said a word.

That night, there was a knock on Richard's door. His father and Mavis were there. Richard asked them to come in. They both looked very nervous. They sat side by side on the couch Dee had given him.

Dan cleared his throat. "Richard, I'm selling the house. As soon as I can sell it, Mavis and I are getting married."

"I know," said Richard.

"I should have told you sooner, son. We haven't told Steve or Pam yet, either. Mavis thought—we thought— We're going to see Pam now. Would you want to come along?"

34

"No, thank you," said Richard.

Mavis got up and walked around the apartment. She looked out the windows. She glanced into Richard's bedroom. She looked at the ceilings and the cupboards. Richard and Grandpa G. had built the cupboards. They were very pretty.

"What about Mother's things?" Richard asked his father. Mavis's face got very red, but she said nothing.

"You kids can divide them," Dan said. "But remember, she did leave you money. Probably Steve and Pam will want some of her things, too."

"Don't you want any of Mother's things?" Richard asked.

Mavis said, "Dan, I'll wait for you in the car." She went down the stairs.

Dan turned to Richard. "I won't need much. I'll be living in Mavis's house. I'll just be taking my radios and things like that."

"Didn't you forget Mom awful quick?" Richard asked.

Dan spun around to face his son. Tears came to his eyes. Richard was always catching him off guard. He spoke very softly. "I'll never forget your mother, Richard. Never." He looked very sad and tired. "Sure you don't want to come along and see Pam? You could get to know Mavis better."

"No, thank you," said Richard again. His father went slowly down the stairs. Richard looked out the window. Mavis was sitting in his father's car. She had her arms folded.

Chapter 6

Holly Would

After his father and Mavis left his apartment, Richard got in his car. He went for a drive.

He came to a small town with a bar. Some of the kids he had gone to school with hung out there. He went in and ordered a beer. It didn't taste good. He didn't like beer. His mother had asked him not to drink, and he never did.

So Richard sat in the bar and listened to the music. A girl named Holly came and sat beside him. He remembered her from school. She had quit school. Holly was pretty. She had long black hair.

"How are you doing, Richard?" she asked.

"OK."

"I heard your mother died."

"Yeah."

"That's too bad. I'm sorry."

"Yeah."

"Do you live with your dad?"

"I've got my own apartment house now."

"You have? A whole house? Well, well."

"Yes, and I have my own car, too."

"Do you really? Well, why don't you take me for a ride?" said Holly, tossing her hair out of her eyes. Richard looked at her. Every time he had asked a girl out, she had said no.

"Would you really go for a ride with me?" he asked.

"Sure, I would. Why not? It's a bore here." She put out her cigarette. Richard did not smoke. His mother wouldn't have liked that.

"OK, let's go," he said.

* * *

Richard took Holly out a lot after that. She liked his car, and she liked the presents he bought for her. He spent a lot of money. He spent all the rent money and still ran short. Holly suggested that he rent the other apartment to get more money. She knew some guys looking for a place.

Holly's friends didn't have enough money for a full month's rent. They gave Richard $50 and moved in. They said they would pay him the rest the next week. Soon, a loud four-wheel-drive pickup and a motorcycle were in the driveway.

Just a few days later, Mrs. Johnson came to the door. She was the nice lady who lived downstairs. "Richard, I'm going to move," she told him. "I don't like the boys who have moved in upstairs. I don't like the way they look or the way they talk. A lot of people go in and out, and there is too much noise."

Richard felt bad for Mrs. Johnson. He didn't want her to lose her home. But he had other things on his mind. He and Holly were having fun. Holly was teaching him lots of things he hadn't known about.

Richard soon forgot about Mrs. Johnson. He made no effort to rent the apartment to anyone else, either.

Richard began to dip into the rest of the money from his mother. It was in a savings account now, and he could take some out whenever he wanted to.

Bills came, and Richard piled them on top of his refrigerator without looking at them. He hadn't paid bills since he met Holly. Letters from the bank came, too, one after another. Richard ignored them, also.

* * *

One day, a Sold sign appeared on Dan Cook's lawn. Soon after that, he and Mavis got married at city hall.

There was a party after the wedding. Richard was invited. He asked Holly to go with him. When Pam saw them come in, she took

40

Richard aside. "Richard, what are you doing here with that girl?" she asked.

"She's my girlfriend," he said.

"Oh, no, Richard! She's not a nice girl."

"She has been nice to me," said Richard.

"She would be. She is nice to a lot of men," said Pam. "Wait until you run out of money, and you'll see how nice she is!"

"I am out of money," replied Richard.

"The rent money *and* Mother's money? How could you have spent all of that?"

Richard didn't answer her. He still had enough of his mother's money left to buy food for a while, if he didn't eat much. But he was too ashamed to tell Pam anything.

Pam lowered her voice, and said, "Richard, you are nothing but a rotten loser!" Then she walked away.

Pam's words hurt Richard a lot. But she was right about Holly. The next day, he told Holly that he was out of money. She said, "What do you mean? You have an apartment house and a nice car. How come you haven't got any money? How can we go out and have fun now?"

"Your friends don't pay their rent," Richard explained. "And the lady downstairs moved out months ago because of them. I'm broke."

Holly stood with her hands on her hips. "Find yourself another girl, Richard. I don't go out with losers." She slammed the door of his apartment as she left.

Richard wasn't surprised that she was gone. Everybody he liked left him. He was used to it.

A week later, Holly's friends moved out in the middle of the night. They left owing five months' back rent. And they took the stove and refrigerator from the apartment.

All the months that Richard had been going with Holly, Dee hadn't had a chance to talk with him. Either Richard was out with Holly, or Holly was at his place. Now, Dee noticed that Holly wasn't around anymore. She went over to see how Richard was doing.

"You're as thin as a rail!" Dee said when Richard opened the door.

Just then, a strange man came up the walk behind Dee. "Are you Richard Cook?" he asked.

"Yes," said Richard.

"This is for you," the man said. He handed Richard a fat envelope. Richard went inside and upstairs. He threw the envelope down on his kitchen table. Dee trailed behind him.

"Aren't you going to open it?" she asked.

"You can," Richard said.

Dee looked at him over the top of her glasses. Then she studied the contents of the envelope. "This is a summons to court! The bank is taking you to court because you haven't kept up your house payments. You're going to lose the house, Richard! Didn't you get any warnings?"

Richard pointed to the top of the refrigerator. Dee took down the stack of neglected bills and letters. She looked them over, one by one.

"The power company is threatening to cut off your gas and lights," she said at last. "But that's not the worst of it. The bank has been warning you for months. Look at this!"

Dee waved one of the letters at Richard. "This came more than a month ago. It told you that you had thirty days to pay up, or they'd go to court. This was a registered letter, Richard. Somebody had to deliver it to you in person. You had to sign your name to get it. And you didn't even open it!"

"I probably couldn't have read it, anyway, Dee," Richard said. "What does it matter? I don't have the money."

"You're going to lose the house."

"I know. I don't care."

"Well, *I* care!" Dee said. "First, I'm going over to the power company. I've got a hundred dollars I can give them so they won't cut off your lights and gas for a while. Have you got enough food here?"

"Thanks, Dee. I'm fine," said Richard.

"And when I get home, I'm going to call that father of yours."

Dee stood and looked at Richard. He had his eyes closed, and he didn't speak to her again.

When Dee got home from talking with the power company, she called Dan Cook. Mavis answered the phone. She said Dan wasn't home. Dee didn't care for Mavis, but she told her the problem and asked her to tell Dan.

"I'll take care of it," said Mavis. "But from now on, I'll thank you not to butt into our family's business."

Mavis did take care of things, in her own way. She told Dan nothing at all about Richard's problem.

Mavis did, however, call her friend Millie Thomas. Millie was the real estate saleswoman who had sold Dan's house. Mavis knew that her friend wanted to buy some rental property for herself.

Richard didn't hear from his father, and he did lose his apartment house.

In the end, there was a public sale at the courthouse. Anyone could make an offer on the house. Millie Thomas managed to buy the apartment house for less than it was worth.

Chapter 7

Moving Around

After Richard lost the apartment house, Dee didn't hear from him for nearly six months. Then one day, he came to see her. He had quite a story to tell.

Richard had moved in with his father and Mavis for a while. He started going to classes that taught students how to build a house.

It didn't take long before Richard and Mavis started having fights. "Mavis didn't want me in her house. Dad just sort of does whatever she says, so I left," Richard said. He didn't stop to explain to Dee where he had moved to.

At the end of the class, there was a job with a carpenter. Richard had done very well in the class. He had learned a lot from Grandpa G. He had started his new job, and in just a week, he was laid off.

"I didn't do anything wrong. Honest, I didn't," he said. "They just ran out of work."

"I do believe you," said Dee. "I'm proud of you for finishing the class. It shows that you can do what you set your mind to."

"Yes, and I got high grades, too."

"Good for you! So where are you living now? Are you back with Dan and Mavis?"

"Are you kidding? I'll never go back there again. When I call to talk to Dad, she says he's out. I guess he thinks it's my fault that I lost my job."

"Well, then, where are you living?" Dee asked.

"With Joe."

"Who is Joe?"

"Joe Carter. I met Joe while I was taking my class. He came to the school looking for a handyman. He runs a foster care home for retarded people. He needed some help around the house. He lets me live there, and I help him. But Joe can't pay me very much. I need another job."

"Have you had any luck finding one?" asked Dee.

"Not yet, but Joe is helping me look."

"Joe sounds like a pretty good guy."

"He is. He's the first real friend I have ever had." Then Richard added, "Except Mom and Grandpa G. and you. By the way, Dee, I'm going to pay you back that hundred dollars. You know, what you spent on my gas and lights."

Dee smiled sadly. "I'm sorry you lost your house, Richard," she said. "When I explained your problem to Mavis, she promised to tell your dad. I thought for sure he would do something."

"I don't think Mavis ever told him," Richard said. "Dad has never said a thing about it."

Dee had to turn her back. She didn't want Richard to see the anger she felt at how badly he had been treated.

"Anyway, it was my fault I lost the house," Richard said. "I spent all my money on a girl that didn't even care about me. I was sure stupid. But back then, I was mixed up and upset."

Dee looked out the window. Richard had driven up in an old pickup truck. "Is that your truck?" she asked.

"Yes, I had to sell my car. I didn't have any money at all."

"Where did you get the truck?" Dee asked.

"Same place I got the car. The man gave me the truck and three hundred dollars for my car."

"How much did you pay for the car in the first place?"

"Two thousand dollars," Richard admitted. Dee said nothing.

Richard smiled at her. "I know it wasn't a good deal. But, Dee, I learned a lot. I know more about money now. Next time, I'll be able to make a better deal."

She turned back and smiled at him then. "Richard, you have had some bad times. But I think you are really growing up now. I always knew you would be a winner."

He grinned. "Yeah, that's what Joe says, too. Well, it's been good to see you. I'd better get back now. Joe and the guys need me to help get supper." He hugged Dee and said good-bye.

After he was gone, Dee thought about all he had told her.

"If only I had known how things would turn out!" she thought. "I would have tried to buy that house myself. Richard could have lived there and worked for me, taking care of the place. I could have helped him."

Looking back, Dee could see that many people had tried to help Richard. His mother had tried. Grandpa G. had tried. At one time, even his father had tried. Maybe it was too much help. Now, Richard would have to help himself.

Dee had to admit one thing. Richard had changed. Maybe he had learned from the mess he had been in. That happened to people sometimes. Maybe he wasn't as slow as people thought.

Chapter 8

Needed: A Job

Joe Carter was sitting at his kitchen table. He and Richard were having a cup of coffee. He said, "Rich, you're good help. Thanks for helping me get the guys to bed. They're a handful for one man!"

Joe had three retarded men that he took care of. John couldn't get dressed without help. Sammy needed help with everything. Ronald couldn't talk much, but he had a paper route. Joe was very good to the men.

"I'm glad to help," said Richard. "I appreciate you letting me stay here."

"You're earning your room and board," replied Joe. "But we need to find you a job. Let's see. What can you do?" He was looking at the newspaper.

"I can't do much of anything right," said Richard.

"Nonsense," said Joe. "Let's make a list of what you can do. Can you drive a car?"

Richard laughed, "You know I can."

"Have you ever had a ticket?"

"No."

"OK, safe driver. That's first on your list. Now, let's see. You can cook and keep house. You're neat and clean. And do you know what I like best about you?"

"No, what?" asked Richard, smiling.

"You are a kind person. I've never seen you be mean to anybody. You don't smoke, drink, or swear. You really are a nice guy."

Richard was very pleased. He hadn't had that much praise in his life.

Joe was looking at the Help Wanted ads. "Here's an ad for you," he said and read it to Richard.

Needed: Male to live in and help elderly gentleman. Some cooking and yard work. Must be able to drive. Good wages plus room and board. Call 726-5000.

When he had finished reading the ad, Joe said, "Rich, I think you're in business!"

Richard called the number listed. The next day, Donald Revson came to see him. He said that his mother had died recently. His father,

Mike, could not live alone in the country. He just needed someone to help him a little. He needed to be taken on errands and to the doctor. The family wanted someone kind that they could trust.

Richard said, "I'd really like to have that job, Mr. Revson."

"What kind of work have you done?" asked Revson.

Richard looked at Joe. What could he say? He had never had a regular job for any length of time. His job as carpenter had lasted such a short time that Richard didn't even count it.

Joe said, "He has been working here for me. This is a foster care home. He has been good help. He is kind to the men I care for. I believe Richard would do a good job for you."

"I want you to meet my father," said Revson. "If Big Mike likes you, you look fine to me. Everyone calls my dad Big Mike."

Donald took Richard to Mike Revson's farm home. Big Mike came to the door. He walked slowly because he had trouble seeing. He wore thick glasses.

Donald Revson introduced Richard to his father. They talked for a while. Richard liked Big Mike right away. He reminded Richard of Grandpa G.

"Do you want to live out here with an old geezer like me?" asked Mike.

"Yes, sir, I do," Richard answered. They shook hands. Richard had his first job.

* * *

Big Mike was easy to live with and work for. Richard cooked him his favorite foods. He kept the house clean and mowed the lawn. He fixed the broken boards on the back porch.

"You'll make someone a good husband one day," said Mike.

"Not me," said Richard. He told Mike about Holly.

"It's a good thing that happened," said Mike. "Now you know a lot more about women. The right girl will come along one day. She will turn your head." Big Mike talked just like Grandpa G.

Mike bought paint, and Richard painted the front porch. Mike sat in his rocking chair and watched. He told Richard stories about his life. He had lived a long time. He had had many adventures. Richard thought it was all interesting.

Donald Revson often stopped by to see his father. "Dad, I'm glad we found Richard for you. He hasn't heard your stories before. You needed a new audience."

Big Mike just chuckled.

At night, Richard and Big Mike played chess. Mike taught him how. "Steve and Dad play chess," Richard told him. "Dad never thought I was smart enough to learn."

"You could surprise them now," said Mike. "What is it, two out of three you have beaten me?"

"It's about time I won at something," said Richard. "Lots of people think I'm a loser."

"You're only a loser when you quit trying," said Mike.

Richard smiled, "That's just what my mother used to say."

"Smart lady, your mother," Mike said. "You must get your spirit from her. Now, let's turn in. I'm tired."

Richard helped Mike get to bed. Then he went to his own room. He lay in the dark, smiling, for a long time.

Mike Revson's birthday arrived. He was 80. Don and his wife came to take Mike out for dinner.

"Why don't you come along to the party?" Mike asked Richard.

Mrs. Revson said, "Yes, Richard, please come. We'd love to have you help celebrate."

Richard ran upstairs. He put on his new shirt and pants. He had bought them with his first paycheck. He looked very nice.

They went to the best restaurant in town. Richard and Big Mike studied the menu.

"I can't read this very well," said Richard.

"I can't see it very well," Mike replied. "That makes us even. So let's order the shrimp. It's very good here."

Everyone laughed. Just then, Richard looked up. His father and Mavis had walked in the door. They stopped still and stared at Richard. They couldn't imagine what Richard was doing with the Revsons. They were very wealthy, well-known people.

The Cooks had to pass the Revson table. They stopped, and Richard stood up. He introduced them to the Revsons. "Dad, Mavis, meet my boss, Big Mike Revson."

It was hard for Big Mike to get up. But he stood and shook hands with Dan. "Mr. Cook, you have a mighty fine son here. He is also quite a chess player. He's a real winner. Beats me all the time."

Dan Cook didn't know what to say. Mavis's face was red again. They said good-bye and went to their table. They hadn't known where Richard was nor what he was doing.

Richard shook Big Mike's hand. "Thanks," he said.

Mike chuckled. "This is a good party, isn't it, boy?"

Later that night, Dan called Richard at Big Mike's house. "Son, I was glad to see you tonight. I've missed you. I'm glad you have a good job."

"Gee, thanks, Dad. I've missed you, too."

"I'd invite you out to the house, but—"

"No, no, that's OK, Dad. But maybe I could buy you a cup of coffee sometime."

"I'd really like that, Richard. I just talked to Steve on the radio and told him I saw you. He said to say hello."

"Hello to him, too. Dad, does Pam still hate me?"

"Son, I don't think she ever hated you. She gets upset and blows off steam sometimes. But don't worry about it. She always cools down."

"I feel better now that we can talk, Dad."

"Me too, Richard. From now on, we'll talk lots. Deal?"

"Deal."

"Good night, Son."

"Good night, Dad."

Chapter 9

Gaining and Losing

Richard had been with Big Mike for eight months. One morning, he fixed eggs and called Mike for breakfast. But Mike didn't come out of his room. Richard called again. No answer. He went to Mike's bedroom door and knocked. Then he opened it.

Mike was still in bed. He moved one hand. Richard could see that something was wrong. Mike tried to speak, but made no sound. One side of his mouth was sagging.

Richard ran for the phone. He called an ambulance. Then he called Donald Revson. The ambulance and Don's car arrived at the same time. Don rode to the hospital in the ambulance with his father. Richard drove Don's car.

Richard sat in the waiting room for hours. Finally, Don came out of his father's room. He drove Richard back to the house. On the way, Don explained what had happened. "Dad has had a stroke. His left side is paralyzed. He can't speak. The doctor says he will live, but he can't come home again. He will need care that you and I can't give him."

Don took his eyes off the road and looked over at Richard. "It isn't fair for you to lose your job like this. I'm really sorry, Richard. But we will have to close up the house."

"Don," said Richard, "don't worry about me. You have enough on your mind. I'm just sorry this had to happen. Mike has been my friend."

"I know," said Don. "You have been his friend, too. And right when he needed you. Thank you for all you have done."

* * *

Richard was again without a job or a home. He tried to call Dee, but she was on vacation. He went to see Joe.

"Buck up, old man," said Joe. "You're just between jobs. It happens to everybody. You can stay here for a while. But it's crowded here right now. Can you sleep on a cot in my room?"

"I don't want to ask my dad for help," Richard replied.

"You won't need to do that, buddy. Something will come along. Just keep trying. Put your name in at the employment office."

That's what Richard did. On the form, under "Job Experience," he wrote: "Took care of old man who couldn't see." The man who interviewed Richard made him mad. He said, "Boy, that must have been a lousy job!" Richard couldn't think of a way to answer him.

That night, Richard talked to Joe. "I don't think I want to take care of an old person again."

"Why not?" asked Joe.

"I get to like them too much. They are my friends, and then something happens to them. Like Grandpa G. and Big Mike. It hurts too much to lose them."

Joe looked at him for a long time. "I know what you mean," he said. "I really loved old Sammy. Then his family moved him to another state. I miss him a lot. I worry about him."

"Then why do you stay in this business?" Richard asked.

"I ask myself one question. I ask myself, 'Joe, did you gain more or lose more?' So far, I have always gained more than I've lost. What about you?"

That night, Richard lay awake on his cot in Joe's room. He thought about Grandpa G. and his mother. He thought about Big Mike. I did gain more than I lost, he thought. Those were the best friends I have ever had. He turned over then and went to sleep.

Within a week, Richard got a call at Joe's. It was Dee, looking for him. "Thanks for sending that money order, Richard. You didn't really have to pay me back that hundred dollars."

"A man has to pay his debts, Dee."

"How are you doing these days?" she asked.

"I'm out of a job again. I'm OK, though. Big Mike helped me open a bank account. I have almost seven hundred dollars saved."

"Good for you!" said Dee. "I'm proud of you. I heard that Mike Revson is in the hospital. I'm sorry. He is a nice man. I'm calling about another job for you. Do you know my friend, Nancy Prentiss? Her father has been in the hospital. He's ready to come home. Nancy's mother can't take care of him alone. They need to hire some help. Would you be interested?"

"How long would they need me?" asked Richard.

"I don't know," Dee answered. "He's an old man. He has been in and out of the hospital a lot. His wife is a tiny little woman. She can't manage him alone. I told them about you. I said that if they could get Richard, they couldn't do better."

"That was nice of you, Dee. Give me their number. I'll call them."

* * *

Richard did go to work for the Prentiss family. The work was so easy that he was bored. Mrs. Prentiss did all of the cooking. A lady came to do the housework. Richard walked Mr. Prentiss to the bathroom. He helped him get to the table for meals. Sometimes, he took the couple for a ride. Mostly, he stayed in his room alone.

Mr. Prentiss was a cross old man. He didn't feel good, and nothing made him happy. Still, it was a good job. Richard was making money. He had no expenses, and he was still saving for a car.

He had an hour off each afternoon. Usually, he went car shopping. He never found anything as good as the red Buick.

"Boy, was I dumb to lose that car!" He said that to himself nearly every day.

Richard went again to the used car lot where he had bought the Buick. The same salesman was there. He and Richard got to be friends. "You've learned a lot about cars, son," the man said.

"I've learned some about dealing, too," said Richard. "So watch out when I'm ready to buy." The man looked at him with new respect.

Other days, Richard would meet Joe at the drugstore. They would have a Coke and talk. Richard learned a lot from Joe. He had good ideas.

One afternoon, Joe said, "Hi, buddy! I've got news. I heard about some classes that are starting. It's in the Community Education Program. There will be free classes in lots of things. There is going to be a meeting in two weeks. Why don't you go?"

"I'd like to," said Richard. "But I can't leave Mr. Prentiss. He's a grouch, and the job is boring. But they need me. And I'm saving for my car."

"I'm really proud of you, Rich. You hang in there, and you have a goal. I think we all need to have goals."

"I don't know what you mean," said Richard.

"I mean that now you are saving to buy a car. That is your dream, your goal. Now, what is your next goal when you have the car?"

"I guess I haven't thought that far," replied Richard.

"OK," said Joe. "Say you have the car. Then what do you want?"

"A place of my own to live. When I had it, I didn't appreciate it. Now, I would. I'm tired of moving here and there."

"That's because you have learned the hard way. Maybe it's the only way to really learn. Now, after you have a car and a place to live, then what?"

"I want a steady job so I can keep my house and car."

"Good, that's another goal," said Joe.

"Then I want to find a nice girl to marry and live with me."

"Whoa, boy!" said Joe. "Next you'll want two kids and a dog."

Joe got up and slapped Richard on the back. "See you, old buddy. Keep in touch."

Richard got excited about his goals. He told Mr. and Mrs. Prentiss about them at supper. Mr. Prentiss smiled. He didn't often do that. He told Richard about when he was a young man. He told him about buying his first car. Mrs. Prentiss blushed when her husband talked about their first date. He also told Richard about how he started his business.

"It must have been hard," said Richard. "It would be hard to earn enough money to buy a place like this."

"Sure, it was hard," Prentiss replied. "We kept working and kept trying." Then he took his wife's hand. "I always had Emma, here, to help me. And she was the prettiest girl in town." Emma Prentiss blushed again.

Richard smiled at them. He tried to picture what they looked like when they were young. He liked the old man better after that night. Old people are really neat when you get to know them, he thought to himself.

Chapter 10

Choices

Mr. Prentiss went in for a checkup the next week. He had to go back to the hospital. The doctor didn't know how long he would be there. Mrs. Prentiss was sad and lonely. She asked Richard to stay on for a week or so. But she needed him only as a driver. He was very bored.

He saw Joe again at the drugstore. "Next Wednesday is the meeting I told you about," said Joe. "How about if we go and see what they have to offer?" Richard agreed to go.

* * *

"We are offering six new classes." Mr. Getts, the community education director, was speaking. "There will be typing, bookkeeping, and woodshop. Then there are three training classes. Training for child care, for teacher's aides, and nurse's aides. Each class leads to employment. We will place you in a job when you finish."

Joe was sitting on Richard's right. On his left was a pretty girl with long blonde hair. Richard looked at her, and she smiled. He turned back to listen to Mr. Getts. For some reason, he felt his face and neck get hot.

Mr. Getts went on, "If you are not willing to complete a class, leave now. If you are not going to work hard, leave now. We are training people for jobs. Don't take up space and time if you are not serious."

Richard stole another look at the blonde. She was sitting quietly with her hands folded. He felt a buzzing in his ears. He had trouble hearing Mr. Getts.

"You can choose the class you want to take," said Getts. "Please choose the thing that you like the best. You will only be happy in a job you like. There are six tables marked with signs. Go to the table of the class you want. Give the clerk there the necessary information. The classes start two weeks from tonight. Thank you for your attention."

People started to buzz and move around the room. Richard sat quietly in his seat.

"What class are you going to take?" The girl next to him had spoken.

Richard turned and looked at her then. She had the bluest eyes he had ever seen. He just gulped and said nothing.

"My name is Mary Paris." She held out her hand.

Still, Richard just looked at her.

Joe spoke up then. "Hi, Mary. I'm Joe Carter. This is my friend Richard Cook." Joe's eyes were dancing.

"Can your friend talk?" she asked, smiling.

"He always could before," laughed Joe.

Richard had barely heard them. Finally, he spoke. "What class are you taking, Mary?"

"Nurse's aide training," said Mary. "I think I want to become a nurse. I figured that this is a good way to find out."

"Me, too," said Richard. "I mean, I think I want to become a nurse, too."

Joe and Mary both laughed then. "You'll probably be the only man in the class," she said.

"I don't care if I am," said Richard. "That's what I'm going to do." He got up then and walked over to the table marked Nurses. Mary followed him and stood in line behind him. He didn't look at her again. He signed the papers with shaking hands. Then he found Joe, and they left together.

"So you're going to be a nurse's aide," said Joe.

"That's right," said Richard.

"Don't you think that was a pretty fast decision? It didn't have anything to do with Mary Paris, did it?"

"No, it didn't, Joe," replied Richard. "My mother and sister both became nurses. I've been taking care of people for a year now. I like that kind of work. That's what I'm going to do."

Richard went back to the Prentiss house. He asked Mrs. Prentiss if he could talk to her.

"Why, of course, Richard," she said. "What can I do for you?"

"I've just been to a meeting. I signed up to take a nurse's aide class. I need a place to stay. The class lasts for six weeks. I know you don't need me here now. But could I stay while I go to school?"

"My goodness, Richard, that's a good idea. I believe it might work out just fine. I didn't know what to do. We need you if my husband comes home. And I can't afford to pay you if he stays in the hospital. It's hard to find a nice young man like you. Yes, please stay here and go to school."

"I won't accept any money while I'm in school," said Richard.

"Then it's a deal. We can help each other," replied Emma Prentiss.

Chapter 11

Study Partners

Richard never thought two weeks could go so slowly. The time until classes started dragged by. He had decided what he wanted to do. Now, he couldn't wait to get started.

At last, the first class night came. As he went in the room, he saw that Mary had been wrong. There were two other men in the class. There were seven women, but Mary was not there.

Sitting behind the desk was a nurse in a white uniform and cap. Beside her was a tall young man. He wore a white coat. He stood up and started to speak. "I'm Jim Fisk. I'm a hospital orderly. This is Mrs. Longhorne. She is a registered nurse. We will be your teachers for this nursing class."

Jim came around to the front of the desk. He leaned against it and looked at the group. "Folks, I want to have a little talk with you. All of us have been or will be sick at some time. It is a time in our lives when we lose control. By that, I mean we are in a weakened condition. We are not able to take care of ourselves. That is scary. We are at the mercy of people who take care of us. Sick people have to be cared for. They must be fed and bathed. Their body wastes must be disposed of. They need medicine and exercise.

"More than that, they need kindness, understanding, and love. Those are maybe the most important things they need. Remember when your mother kissed the sore spot to make it better? Did the kiss make it better?"

Everyone laughed.

"Of course it did," Jim said. "You ran back to your play feeling better. In some ways, we never grow up. A little bit of TLC makes things better. That's tender, loving care. It doesn't matter if you are seven or seventy when you're sick. TLC is what you need. Mrs. Longhorne and I have a good reputation as a team. We turn out good nurse's aides and orderlies. Our people know how to do their jobs. Besides that, we teach people to care about people."

Richard felt warm inside. He remembered the people who cared for his mother. He remembered the kind doctor when Grandpa G. died. He thought about Big Mike.

Mrs. Longhorne stood up then. She held up a book. "This is the textbook for the class. For the first three weeks, you will be reading a lot. You will take tests on what you read. Then you will be practicing on each other."

Richard's heart sank. He could read better than he used to. But he was still a very slow reader. There were many words he did not understand.

Mrs. Longhorne continued. "I suggest you work together and help each other. You will work in teams with a study partner. We will take a short break now. Get your book, and select your partner."

Richard stood. He walked out of the classroom and out of the building. He stood on the steps and felt sick. He had really looked forward to the training program. He slowly went down the steps. He kicked a stone ahead of him on the sidewalk. He walked with his head down, hands in his pockets.

Someone hurrying up the walk bumped into him.

"Oh, I'm sorry. I'm late. Has the class started yet?" It was Mary Paris.

"Yeah," Richard said. "It's started."

"Then where are you going?" Mary asked.

"I'm going to drop out."

"Drop out? You haven't even started yet."

"No, and I'm not going to," said Richard.

"Why not? I thought you were sure you wanted nursing."

"You want to know why? You really want to know?" Richard spoke with anger in his voice. "I'll tell you why. I can't read good enough, that's why! There is a book *this thick!* And we have to have study partners. Who would want me for a partner?"

Mary stood looking at him. "You aren't the only one with a problem," she said. "I'm late because I had to wait for my dad to bring me. I can't drive. I'll probably miss classes because of it. I'll probably get kicked out. Maybe they won't even let me start tonight."

"Why can't you drive?" asked Richard.

"It's a long story. I was in an accident when I was sixteen. I was hurt pretty bad. Now, I'm afraid. I just can't get behind a wheel. Even if I get to the classes, I don't know how I'd get to work."

They both sat down on the steps. She looked very discouraged. "I'll bet I could help you learn to drive," Richard said. "In a few days, I'm going to buy a car."

"Well, I can read all right," said Mary. "I'll bet I could help you with the reading. I'll tell you what. If you will pick me up for class, we can be study partners. You drive, I'll read."

That made him smile. She wanted the class as badly as he did. And she had a problem, too. He was sure he could teach her to drive. Besides, he had never seen such blue eyes. "Shake, partner," he said. And they went into the building together.

Chapter 12

Life Partners

The six weeks of the nursing class flew by.

Richard and Mary went car shopping. He bought a small car that would be easy for her to drive. Every afternoon after class, they studied together. Then they would go for a drive. When she felt ready, Mary got behind the wheel.

With Mary's help, Richard was able to keep up with the reading for the class. Even the tests weren't too hard for him. He passed every one.

One of the things the class did was to go on field trips. They visited the places where jobs were available. They saw two hospitals. They saw a home for retarded children. They visited local nursing homes. The last week, they were asked to make a choice about where they wanted to work.

Richard and Mary had grown very close. Jim Fisk teased them about holding hands in class.

"When I spoke of TLC, I meant for the patients," he laughed. He was standing at the curb, talking to them. Mary was behind the wheel of Richard's car. "Have you two decided where you want to work yet?" Jim asked.

"Yes," said Richard. "We have both applied at Golden Valley Nursing Home."

"Any particular reason you want nursing home work?" asked Jim.

"For me," said Richard, "it was my grandfather. He was my good friend. And Big Mike Revson is at Golden Valley. I really like those guys. People their age are just like us, only older and wiser. They get very lonely, and I want to be with them."

"For me," said Mary, "it was my Gram. My Grandmother Paris took care of me after my accident. Until then, I had never taken the time to know her very well. She's wonderful. Maybe someday she will be unable to care for herself. She may be in a nursing home. I would want someone like me to take care of her."

"Pretty good reasons, I'd say," Jim remarked. "You two look like a couple of winners to me."

"We are winners," said Richard. He squeezed Mary's hand. "And we want to work together."

"Yes, I can see that," said Jim, smiling.

Graduation was on a bright October day. Jim Fisk and Mrs. Longhorne gave Richard and Mary their nursing pins. They shook hands.

Jim said, "Good luck. Let us hear from you." He watched them walk out of the classroom. Richard's arm was around Mary.

Jim did hear from Richard and Mary. He read about them in the local paper.

Daily Press — March 3
Cook-Paris Engagement
Mr. and Mrs. Walter Paris announce the engagement of their daughter, Mary, to Richard Cook. Richard's parents are Dan Cook and the late Carol Cook. A June wedding is planned.

Cook-Paris Wedding

Mary Paris and Richard Cook were united in marriage June 10. The scene of the wedding was the dining room of the Golden Valley Nursing Home. Rev. John Williams performed the ceremony.

Attending the bride was her grandmother, Sarah Paris. The best man was Mike Revson. A reception and dinner followed the ceremony.

Wedding guests, besides the families of the couple, were: Dee Spencer, Joe Carter, Mr. and Mrs. Donald Revson, Emma Prentiss, Jim Fisk, Alice Longhorne, and residents of the Golden Valley home. After a short honeymoon, the couple plan to return to this city, where they are both employed at the Golden Valley Nursing Home.

Letters to the Editor

There was a lovely wedding last week. Mary Paris and Richard Cook got married. Mary is a nurse's aide at the Golden Valley Nursing Home. Richard is an orderly there. The couple wanted to invite Golden Valley people to their wedding. But they were not able to come. So Richard and Mary took the wedding to them.

This was a bright and happy day for many elderly people. For three months, they looked forward to the wedding. Mrs. Pratt, retired music teacher, played the Wedding March. The cake was decorated by Muriel Daniels. She owned a bakery for 50 years. Everyone helped to decorate the dining room.

There were many lovely gifts made by the residents. There was a painting by Frieda Glutz. Mrs. Glutz is a well-known painter who retired recently. "Big Mike" Revson was the best man, and he furnished the ring.

My hat is off to these young people. They shared their special day. They brought back happy memories to so many. We at Golden Valley thank them. We wish them many happy years together.

Elizabeth Wolfe, Director
Golden Valley Nursing Home

Seven series of good books for all readers:

WRITERS' VOICES
Selections from the works of America's finest and most popular writers, along with background information, maps, and other supplementary materials. Authors include: Kareem Abdul-Jabbar • Maya Angelou • Bill Cosby • Alex Haley • Stephen King • Loretta Lynn • Larry McMurtry • Amy Tan • Anne Tyler • Abigail Van Buren • Alice Walker • Tom Wolfe, and many others.

NEW WRITERS' VOICES
Anthologies and individual narratives by adult learners. A wide range of topics includes home and family, prison life, and meeting challenges. Many titles contain photographs or illustrations.

OURWORLD
Selections from the works of well-known science writers, along with related articles and illustrations. Authors include David Attenborough and Carl Sagan.

FOR YOUR INFORMATION
Clearly written and illustrated works on important self-help topics. Subjects include: Eating Right • Managing Stress • Getting Fit • About AIDS • Getting Good Health Care, among others.

TIMELESS TALES
Classic myths, legends, folk tales, and other stories from around the world, with special illustrations.

SPORTS
Fact-filled books on baseball, football, basketball, and boxing, with lots of action photos. With read-along tapes narrated by Phil Rizzuto, Frank Gifford, Dick Vitale, and Sean O'Grady.

SULLY GOMEZ MYSTERIES
Fast-paced detective series starring Sully Gomez and the streets of Los Angeles.

WRITE FOR OUR FREE COMPLETE CATALOG:

Signal Hill Publications
P.O. Box 131
Syracuse, NY 13210-0131